MW01616193

Tales of a Fourth Grade Nothing

Judy Blume

STUDENT PACKET

NOTE:

The trade book edition of the novel used to prepare this guide is found in the Novel Units catalog and on the Novel Units website. Using other editions may have varied page references.

Please note: We have assigned Interest Levels based on our knowledge of the themes and ideas of the books included in the Novel Units sets, however, please assess the appropriateness of this novel or trade book for the age level and maturity of your students prior to reading with them. You know your students best!

ISBN 978-1-56137-709-1

To order, contact your local school supply store, or:

Toll-Free Fax: 877.716.7272
Phone: 888.650.4224
3901 Union Blvd., Suite 155
St. Louis, MO 63115

sales@novelunits.com

novelunits.com

Activity: To use mathematics and visual perceptual skills

Triangles

"I won Dribble at Jimmy Fargo's birthday party. I won him because I guessed there were three hundred and forty-eight jelly beans in Mrs. Fargo's jar." (page 1)

How many triangles are in the picture below? Be sure you count all sizes of triangles.

Answer: _____

If you are interested in doing so, you may divide these triangles into smaller triangles. It is suggested that you keep track of the number of triangles as they are made. These may then be added to the answer above.

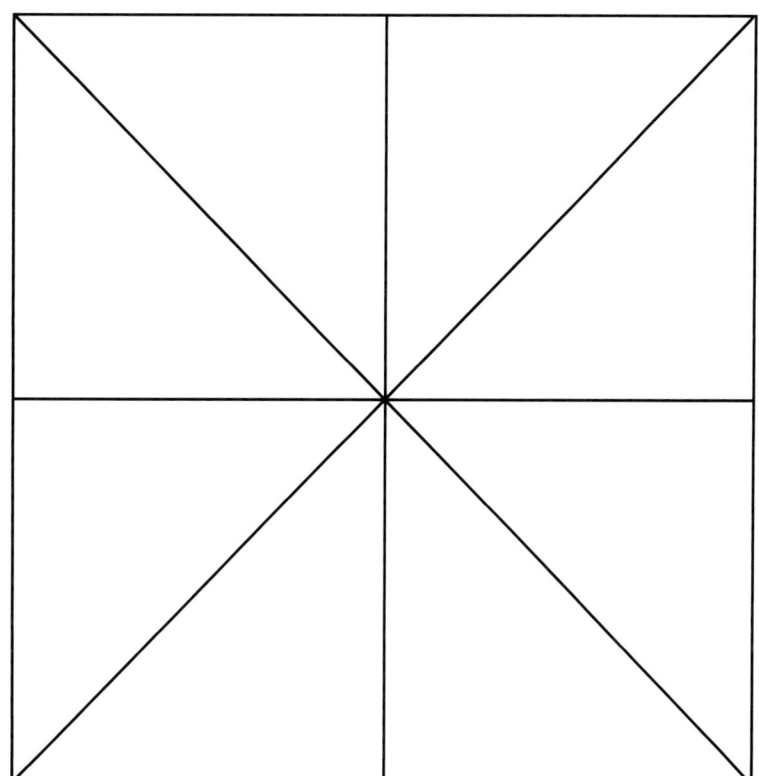

Activity: To use visual perceptual skills

Tangram Turtle

"Then Jimmy handed me a glass bowl. Inside there was some water and three rocks. A tiny green turtle was sleeping on the biggest rock." (page 1)

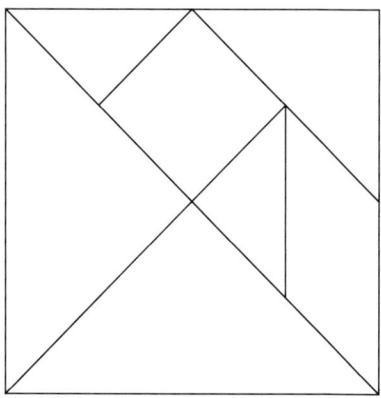

Use the seven pieces of the tangram square to make this turtle. When completed, remove the seven pieces of the tangram square and decorate the turtle. Make something for the turtle out of the tangram pieces. Paste the pieces on another sheet of paper.

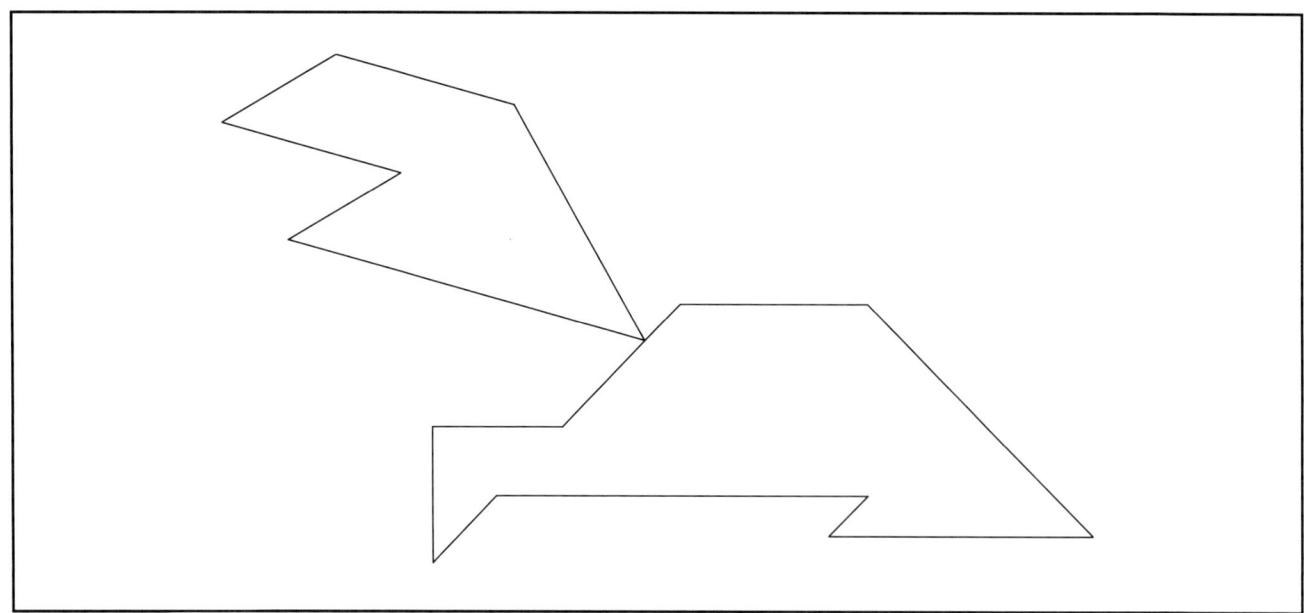

Name_____

Activity: To read for information

Turtles

Turtles are the only reptiles with shells. Most kinds of turtles can pull their heads, legs and tails into their shells, which serve as suits of armor. Few other animals have such excellent natural protection.

Turtles, like all reptiles, are cold-blooded. That means that their body temperatures stay about the same as the temperature of the surrounding air or water.

Turtles cannot be warm and active in cold weather, and so they cannot live in regions that are cold throughout the year. Turtles live in the deserts, forests, grasslands, lakes, marshes, ponds, rivers and seas of the world.

There are approximately 250 species of turtles, about 50 of which live in North America. Turtles vary greatly in size. The largest turtle, the Leatherback Turtle, grows to be from 4 to 8 feet long. In contrast, the common bog turtle measures only about 4 inches in length.

 At one time, pet shops throughout the United States sold thousands of painted turtles and red-eared turtles each year. However, medical researchers discovered that many of these turtles carried bacteria that causes salmonella poisoning, a serious illness in human beings. In 1975, the United States Food and Drug Administration banned the sale of most pet turtles.

Directions: Read the following statements. Mark each either [T] True or [F] False.

1. Turtles are the only reptiles with shells. _____
2. Turtles, like all reptiles, are warm-blooded. _____
3. Turtles cannot live in regions that are cold throughout the year. _____
4. Some turtles live in the sea. _____
5. There are approximately 250 species of turtles. _____
6. All turtles are about the same size. _____
7. The sale of most turtles as pets is banned in the United States. _____
8. Some turtles carry a bacteria that is harmful to human beings. _____

Name_____

Activity: To use imagination

The Best Elevator

"It's an old apartment building. But it's got one of the best elevators in New York City. There are mirrors all around. ...There's a soft, cushioned bench to sit on if you're too tired to stand." (page 2)

What would you do to make the elevator even better? Draw a sketch of the elevator, and include the changes you would make. Describe your changes in writing, and tell why you would make them.

_____

_____

_____

_____

_____

_____

_____

_____

_____

_____

_____

_____

_____

_____

_____

Name_____

Activity: To use reasoning skills

Fudge

"My biggest problem is my brother, Farley Drexel Hatcher. He's two-and-a-half years old. Everybody calls him Fudge." (page 4)

These are synonyms for the word **FUDGE** from *The Doubleday Roget's Thesaurus in Dictionary Form.*

nonsense	foolishness	hogwash	humbug
twaddle	gibberish	rubbish	babbling
prattle	hem and haw	straddle	stall

Webster's Ninth New Collegiate Dictionary defines <u>fudge</u> as: (1) To exceed proper bounds or limits, to exaggerate; foolish nonsense; (2) a soft creamy candy.

Why do you think Farley Drexel Hatcher is nicknamed Fudge? Look at the synonyms and definitions to give you some ideas.

_____

_____

Can you think of a different nickname for him? What would it be and why would you make that choice?

If Fudge were my brother, I'd call him _____ **because**

_____

_____

_____

_____

Activity: To use reasoning skills

Pots and Pans

"She used so many pots and pans Fudge didn't have any left to bang together. And that's one of his favorite pastimes—banging pots and pans together." (pages 6–7)

Do you remember when you were very young? Did you like to bang pots and pans together?

Why do you think it is that most young children like to bang pots and pans together and that most adults allow them to do it? Record your opinions below.

I think that most young children like to bang pots and pans together because: _____

_____

_____

_____

_____

I think that most adults allow young children to bang pots and pans together because: _____

_____

_____

_____

_____

_____

_____

_____

Name_____

Activity: To plan a dinner menu

Company Is Coming!

"Mom spent the day in the kitchen. She really cooked up a storm." (page 6)

Mr. and Mrs. Yarby will be at the Hatcher apartment that evening. Mrs. Hatcher has prepared a special dinner. Think about your favorite dinner. Would you serve your favorite to special company? Make out a dinner menu of the foods that you would serve to the Yarbys if they came to visit you. Choose one item on your menu, and give directions for its preparation. On the back of your paper, do the same thing for a favorite breakfast or lunch.

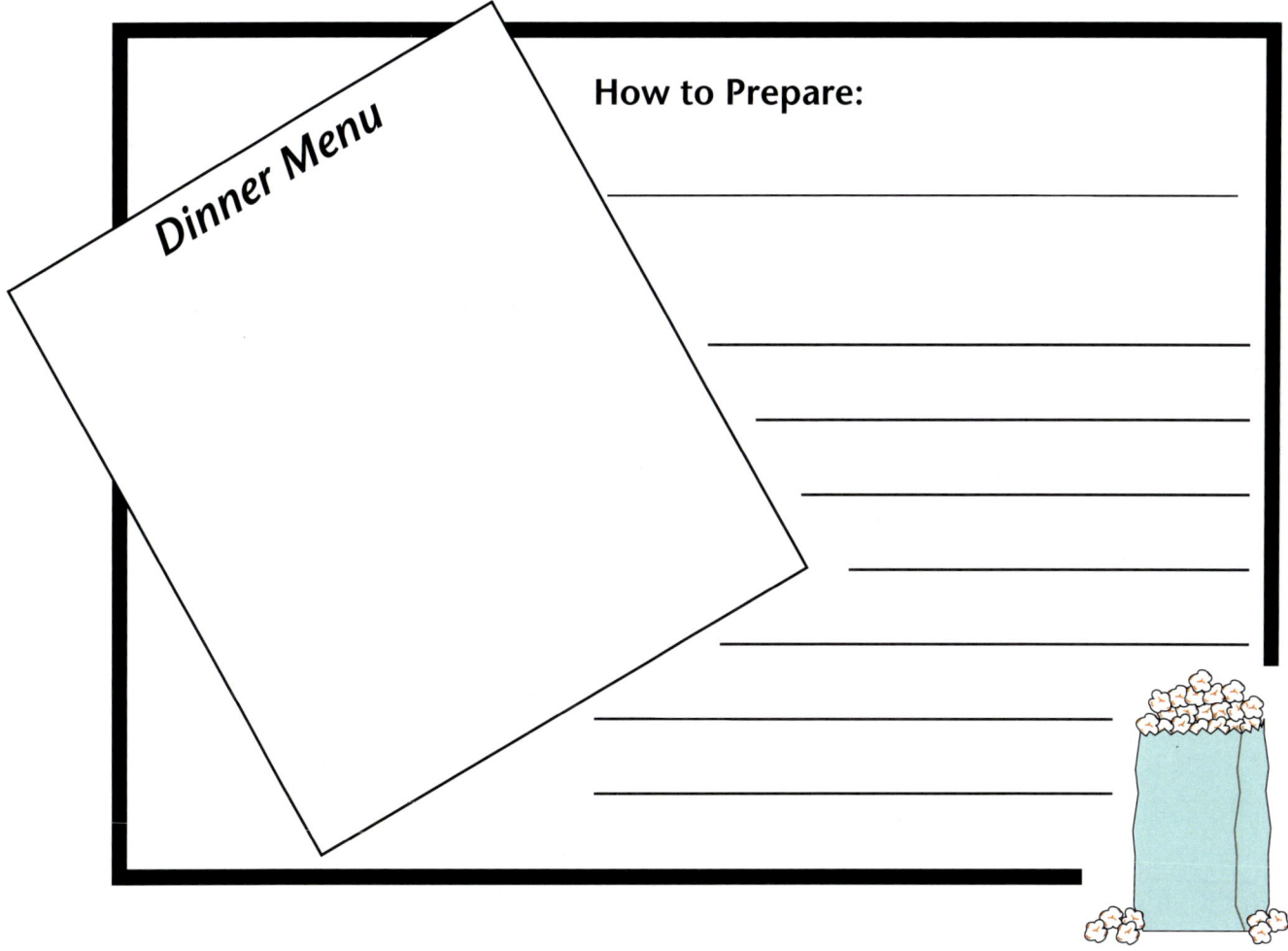

Activity: To do research; to make a poster

No More Flowers!

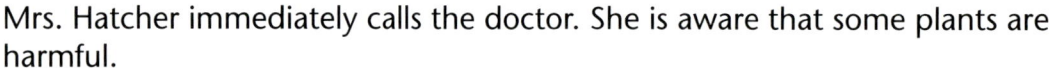

"My mother picked [Fudge] up and forced his mouth open. She fished out a rose petal." (page 8)

Mrs. Hatcher immediately calls the doctor. She is aware that some plants are harmful.

Warning! *Some plants are poisonous or can harm you in other ways.*
Most often the symptoms caused by a "bad" plant are: burning pain in the mouth and throat, blistering, intense thirst, abdominal pain, colic and diarrhea.

Several injurious plants are often used as decorative plants in gardens, homes and offices. Some of the plants the American Medical Association includes on their list of *Plants Producing Systemic Poisoning* are:

Amaryllis	Caladium	Philodendron	Iris
Aloe	Anemone	Hydrangea	Digitalis
Narcissus	Dieffenbachia	Rhododendron	Wisteria

Choose one plant that you are familiar with, or that you want to know more about. Do some research. **Find out why** the plant of your choice is harmful. Make a poster that warns others of the particular consequences of eating some of that plant. **List below the titles, authors, publishers, and copyright dates** of the reference materials you used to find out more about your plant. (Use at least two references.)

Author	Title	Publisher	© date

Activity: To make choices and recommendations

Nice Books

"A nice book would have been a good idea, but a picture dictionary!"
(page 11)

Peter is given a big picture dictionary by Mrs. Yarby. This is the kind of book that he liked when he was four years old. What books do you think would be good choices for Peter? Give the titles, authors, and brief summaries of three books you would recommend that Mrs. Yarby consider as a gift for Peter.

Title: _____
Author: _____
Summary: _____
_____
_____

Title: _____
Author: _____
Summary: _____
_____
_____

Title: _____
Author: _____
Summary: _____
_____
_____

Activity: To create a jingle

Juicy–O

"It'll be Juicy–O! That's all we ever drink. Good for your health!" (page 12)

When companies want to sell a product or a service they often advertise with a catchy <u>jingle</u> or <u>slogan</u> so that people will really remember the product. <u>Jingles</u> are poems that have an obvious easy rhythm with simple repetitions or sounds. The catchy quality of a jingle often stays in the heads of the listeners when it is heard repeatedly. This is just what the advertiser wants. Jingles or slogans can be sung, chanted or recited.

Directions: Create a jingle and a slogan for Juicy–O. Then, on separate paper, create a jingle and a slogan for one of your favorite products or a product of your imagination.

For example:

Jingle
What's got the flavor that you like?
Whether at breakfast or on a hike?
It's Juicy–O! — How do you know?
It's so yummy, it's Juicy–O, it's Juicy–O!

Slogan:
If it's yummy in your tummy, it's Juicy–O!

Your Jingle for Juicy-O:	Your Slogan for Juicy-O:

12

Name_____

Activity: To list characteristics of an object suitable for a specific purpose

Surprise!

To get Fudge to drink the milkshake, Grandma tells him that if he does, he'll find a surprise in the bottom of the glass. Unfortunately, all Fudge sees is the bottom of an empty glass. List some characteristics of an object that **could have been** put in the bottom of the glass.

It would have to be:

waterproof _____ _____ _____

Why do you think Grandma didn't put anything in the glass?

_____

_____

What is another way Grandma could have convinced Fudge to drink the milkshake?

_____

_____

If you were Fudge, how would you have felt? What would you have done?

_____

_____

Draw a picture to tape to the bottom of the glass on the outside.

Activity: To make and defend a choice

No Eat...No Eat!

"Fudge messed around with his cereal for a minute. Then he looked at my father and said, 'NO EAT ... NO EAT ... NO EAT!' " (page 24)

Think of one food that you do not like, and that you would refuse to eat if it was served to you. Defend your refusal with at least three good reasons.

I would refuse to eat _____

because _____

_____

_____

_____

_____

_____

If someone told me to "eat it or wear it," this is how I would look wearing it:

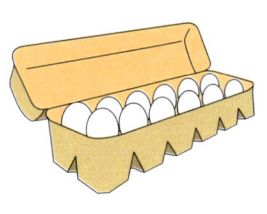

Activity: To make and defend a choice

No Eat...No Eat!

"Fudge messed around with his cereal for a minute. Then he looked at my father and said, 'N
... NO EAT ... NO EAT!' " (page 24)

Think of one food that you do not like, and that you would refuse to eat if it was served t
you. Defend your refusal with at least three good reasons.

I would refuse to eat _____

because _____

_____

_____

_____

_____

_____

If someone told me to "eat it or wear it," this is how I would look wearing it:

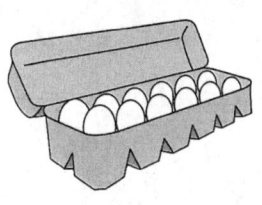

Activity: To make and defend a choice

No Eat...No Eat!

"Fudge messed around with his cereal for a minute. Then he looked at my father and said, 'N...
... NO EAT ... NO EAT!' " (page 24)

Think of one food that you do not like, and that you would refuse to eat if it was served to you. Defend your refusal with at least three good reasons.

I would refuse to eat _____

because _____

_____

_____

_____

_____

_____

If someone told me to "eat it or wear it," this is how I would look wearing it:

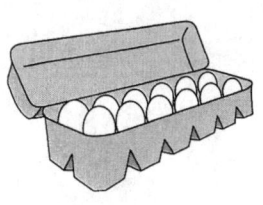

Activity: To make a comparison; to do research

New York City

"I've never been mugged. But sooner or later I probably will be. My father's told me what to do. Give the muggers whatever they want and try not to get hit on the head." (page 27)

Because of its large population, more crimes are committed in New York City than any other city in the United States. However, the **crime rate**—the number of crimes committed for every 100,000 residents—is actually **lower** in New York than in many other cities.*

New York's crime and drug addiction problems are closely related. About half of the drug addicts in the United States live in New York City. They commit many of the city's burglaries and attacks on individuals to get money for drugs.*

What is the crime rate in your community? Is there a crime and/or drug prevention program? Find out from your local law enforcement agency. Compare your community to New York City in the areas listed below. (If you live in New York City, compare it to another city of your choice.)

New York City	**My Community**
more crime than any other U.S. city	_____
high crime rate	rate of_____crimes per_____
large population of drug addicts	_____
$4 billion/year on welfare programs	_____
1-1/2 million people living in poverty	_____
serious racial conflicts	_____

* <u>Source:</u> *Information Finder, 1994 World Book, Inc.*

Activity: To make a personal statement using a limerick

NOBODY!

"Taking dope is even dumber than smoking, so nobody's going to hook me!" (p. 28)

Peter makes a definite statement about the use of drugs and about smoking. What else should you do or NOT do to have a healthy body?

no drugs   _____   _____

no smoking   _____   _____

Use the <u>limerick</u> poetry form to state your personal feelings about the health of your body. In a <u>limerick</u> lines 1, 2 and 5 rhyme, and lines 3 and 4 rhyme. For example:

Smoking is dumb. Taking dope is dumber,
So don't get caught in a deep slumber.
You don't have to be wealthy
To keep your body healthy.
Be strong! Be more than a number!

Your limerick:

_____ 1

_____ 2

_____ 3

_____ 4

_____ 5

Name_____

Activity: To investigate local environmental pollution

Leaves

"I never saw bright red, yellow, and orange leaves until the day my father took us for a drive in the country. The reason the leaves don't turn bright colors in New York is the air pollution." (page 29)

Environment: All of the surroundings of a living thing.

Pollution: Any human-caused change in the environment that creates an undesirable effect on living and non-living things.

How polluted is **YOUR** environment? Consider your community. Describe:

Noise:_____

_____

_____

Litter:_____

_____

_____

Trash:_____

_____

_____

Other:_____

_____

_____

Do you think your environment is polluted? Give reasons for your reply. Use the back of the page to write your answer.

17

Activity: To use mathematics skills; to learn more about the environment.

Your Environment
What can YOU do to help?

Think about this: ON THE AVERAGE, EACH PERSON IN THE UNITED STATES DISCARDS ABOUT 3 1/2 POUNDS OF SOLID WASTE DAILY.

Using 3 1/2 pounds daily, how much is discarded per person in a week? _____In 31

days? _____ In 365 days? _____

Paper and paper products make up about 50% of the solid waste. Using the figures above, and the fact that paper and paper products make up 50% of the solid waste, what would be the weight of the paper and paper products discarded per person in:

one week? _____ 31 days? _____ 365 days? _____

Make a list of things that YOU can do to cut down on this figure of 3 1/2 pounds/day. REMEMBER: Recycling paper reduces the pressure on our forests for wood pulp, so less logging is necessary.

To cut down on the amount of garbage and trash that I discard, I will:

_____

_____

_____

_____

_____

_____

_____

Name_____

Activity: To match words with definitions; to learn more about pollution

Pollution Crossword Puzzle

Directions: Match these pollution-related words to their meanings by correctly filling in the crossword puzzle:

CONSUME	ENERGY	ENVIRONMENT	GARBAGE
LITTER	POLLUTE	RECYCLE	REDUCE
REUSE	SOLID WASTE	TRASH	UNSAFE

Across

1. all the surroundings of a living thing
3. food that is thrown away
5. to use up something
6. to make smaller
7. dangerous
9. solid waste that has not been properly disposed of
10. to make the environment unsightly, unhealthy or unsafe

Down

1. the ability to do work; power
2. all solid waste except garbage
4. to collect used products to make into new products
6. to use again
8. trash and garbage (two words)

Activity: To use the letters of one word to form others; spelling practice

Playground

"Why don't you take Fudge over to the playground? Then I'll know where to find you."
(page 32)

Mrs. Hatcher leaves Fudge at the playground in Central Park with Sheila, Peter and Jimmy. In three minutes, how many words can you make from the letters in the word PLAYGROUND? Make a list.

PLAY   _____   _____

GROUND   _____   _____

DAY   _____   _____

_____   _____   _____

_____   _____   _____

_____   _____   _____

Compare you list of words with that of another member of the group. Could you have made a longer list by working together? Work together to do the following:

In three minutes, make as many words as you can from the letters in CENTRAL PARK. (Use the back of the page if you run out of lines.)

_____   _____   _____

_____   _____   _____

_____   _____   _____

_____   _____   _____

Activity: To follow non-verbal directions

Fudge's Birthday Party Hat

"Grandma put a party hat on each kid's head. Sam screamed...but the others wore their hats and didn't complain." (page 43)

Make a hat for the birthday party. You will need one full newspaper page and a stapler or some tape. You may want to decorate your finished hat with crayons, paint, or colored paper scraps.

Fold the newspaper sheet in half, crosswise. Fold corners A and B to meet at the center.

1.

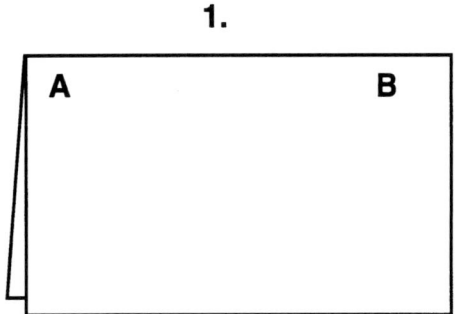

2.

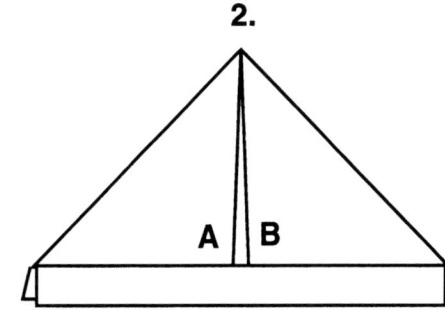

Fold up the bottom edges. (Staple, tape or fold over each of the outside corners, C and D.)

3.

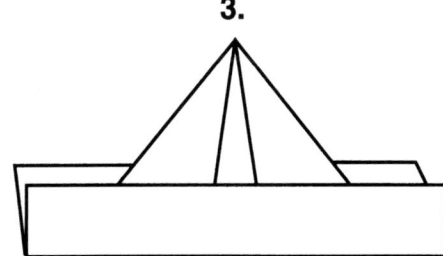

4.

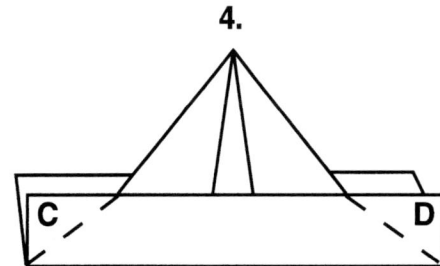

Activity: To follow directions and to make a recommendation

Party Dough

"We've still got half an hour left and I don't know what to do with them anymore." (page 49)

Mrs. Hatcher is desperate! Try this activity and then decide if it is something Mrs. Hatcher should do with Fudge and his party guests.

FIRST: WASH AND DRY YOUR HANDS

Materials:
1/2 cup peanut butter
1/2 cup non-fat dry milk
1 bowl
section of newspaper
large spoon

Process:
  a) Cover work area with newspaper.
  b) Measure the peanut butter and nonfat milk into the bowl.
  c) With your hands, knead and mix the ingredients thoroughly.
  e) Model and experiment with the dough.
  f) This dough is edible. It will keep in a covered container in the refrigerator.
  g) The dough does not harden the way modeling clay would, but putting your creations in the refrigerator will help.
  h) Clean up the work area.

Should Mrs. Hatcher try this with the children? What do you think would happen?

_____

_____

_____

_____

_____

Name_____

Activity: To make a tetrahedron

Party Favor

"Finally the doorbell rang. It was two-thirty. The party was over. I could hardly believe it. I was beginning to think it would never end." (page 51)

Make a **tetrahedron**, a form that has four equilateral triangles as its sides. (Mrs. Hatcher could use this as a party favor for the guests to take home. Something may be placed inside the tetrahedron before it is taped or glued.)

Cut out on outside unbroken lines. The broken lines are the points at which the shape must be folded accurately. The tabs are folded down toward the inside of the shape. Tape or glue in place.

What would you place inside as a party favor? _____

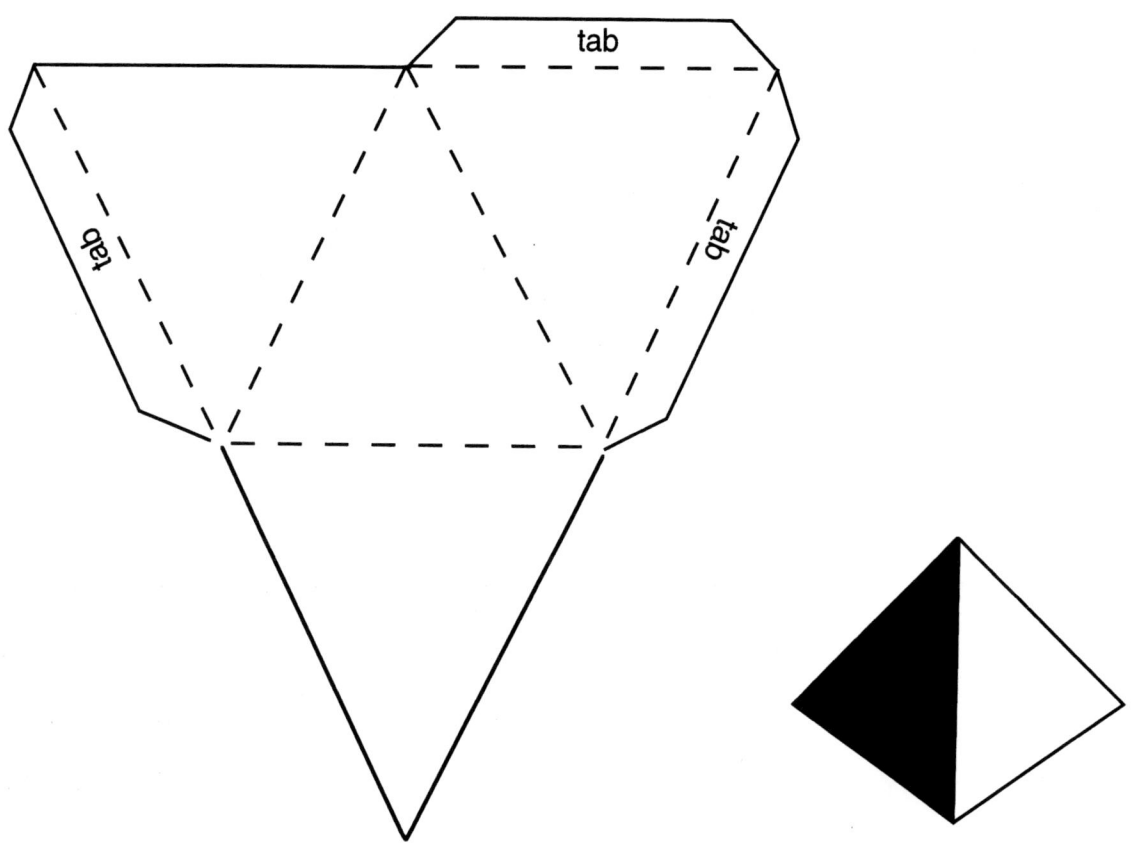

Name_____

Activity: To show appreciation in an original way

To the Dentist

"On Saturday we had to go to the dentist. Dr. Brown is an old friend of my father's." (page 54)

How do you behave when you go to the dentist? Are you more like Peter or Fudge?

How do you feel as you wait to see the dentist?

Have you ever thanked your dentist for helping you to take good care of your teeth and mouth?

A **token of appreciation** is a small gift you can give someone to show them you realize how helpful they have been to you. It doesn't have to be expensive. It is simply a way to express your thoughts and feelings. Have you ever received a token of appreciation? If so, what was it?

Make some token of appreciation for your dentist. Have it ready for your next visit. You may want to make a card, write a letter or a poem, paint a picture, or do something else. Your dentist helps **you** take good care of **you**! Describe below the token of appreciation you decide to make for your dentist:

Is there someone else in your life for whom you'd like to make a token of appreciation? Who? What will you make?

Activity: To create a new brand of shoes

New Shoes

"We headed for Bloomingdale's, where we get our shoes." (page 59)

Imagine that the shoe salesman, Mr. Berman, has a new brand of shoes to show Mrs. Hatcher and the boys. Imagine that **you** are the creator of this new brand of shoes. These shoes are unique. No one has ever thought of making shoes quite like these. These shoes will probably make you famous!

What is the name of your new brand of shoes? _____

What is special about these shoes? _____

_____

Describe the shoes. _____

_____

_____

_____

Draw a picture of one of the shoes:

Name_____

Activity: To use visual perceptual skills

Tangram Sailboat

Sheila said, "I'll write my ten pages on the history of transportation in the city." (pages 71–72)

How were large sailboats used in commerce long ago? They were used to _____

_____

Use the seven pieces of the tangram square to make this large sailboat.

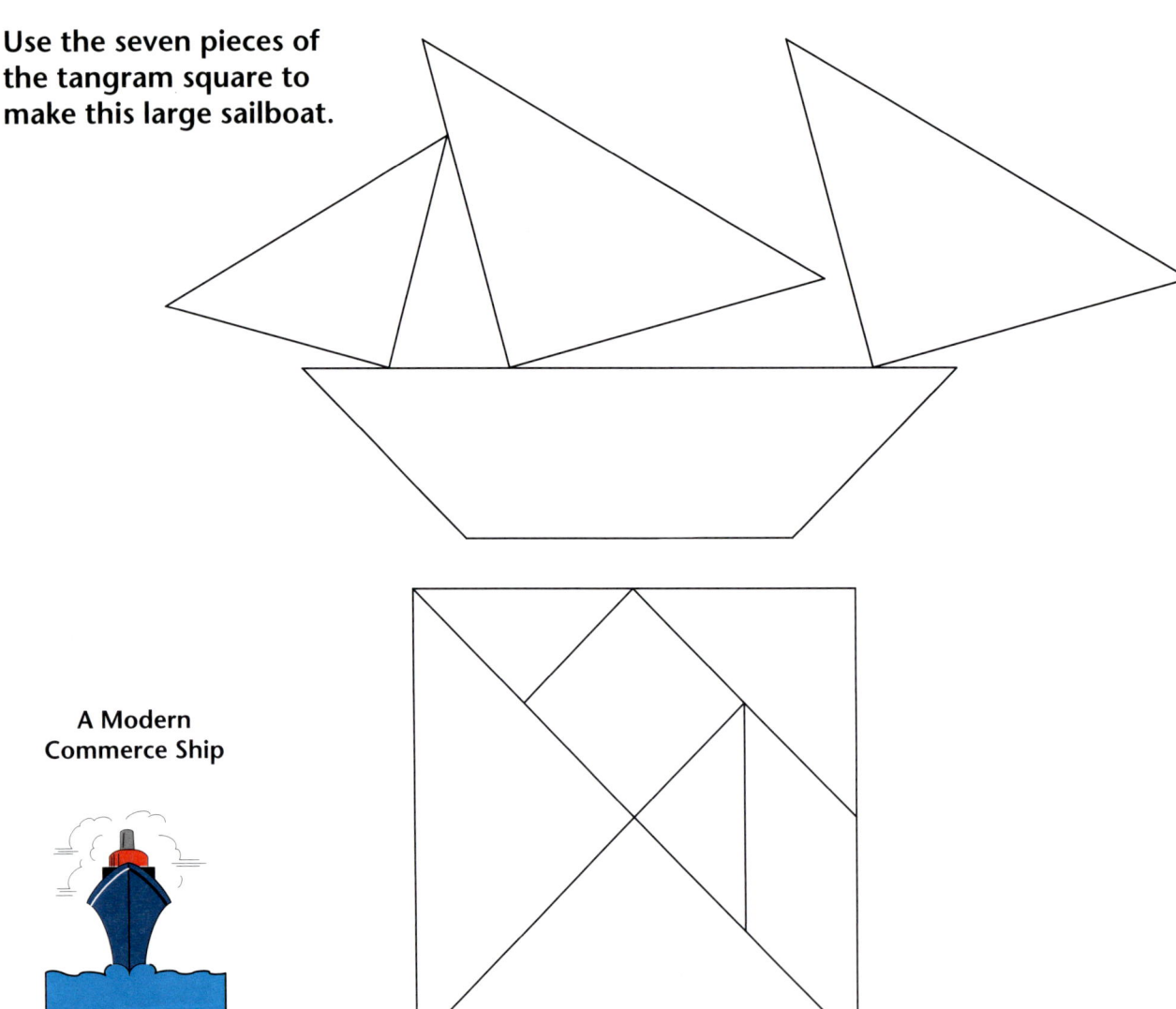

A Modern Commerce Ship

Name_____

Activity: To use visual perceptual skills

Tangram Jet

"Me and Jimmy designed the whole poster ourselves....We divided a chart into land, sea, and air and we planned an illustration for each—with the airplane done in silver sparkle..." (pages 72–73)

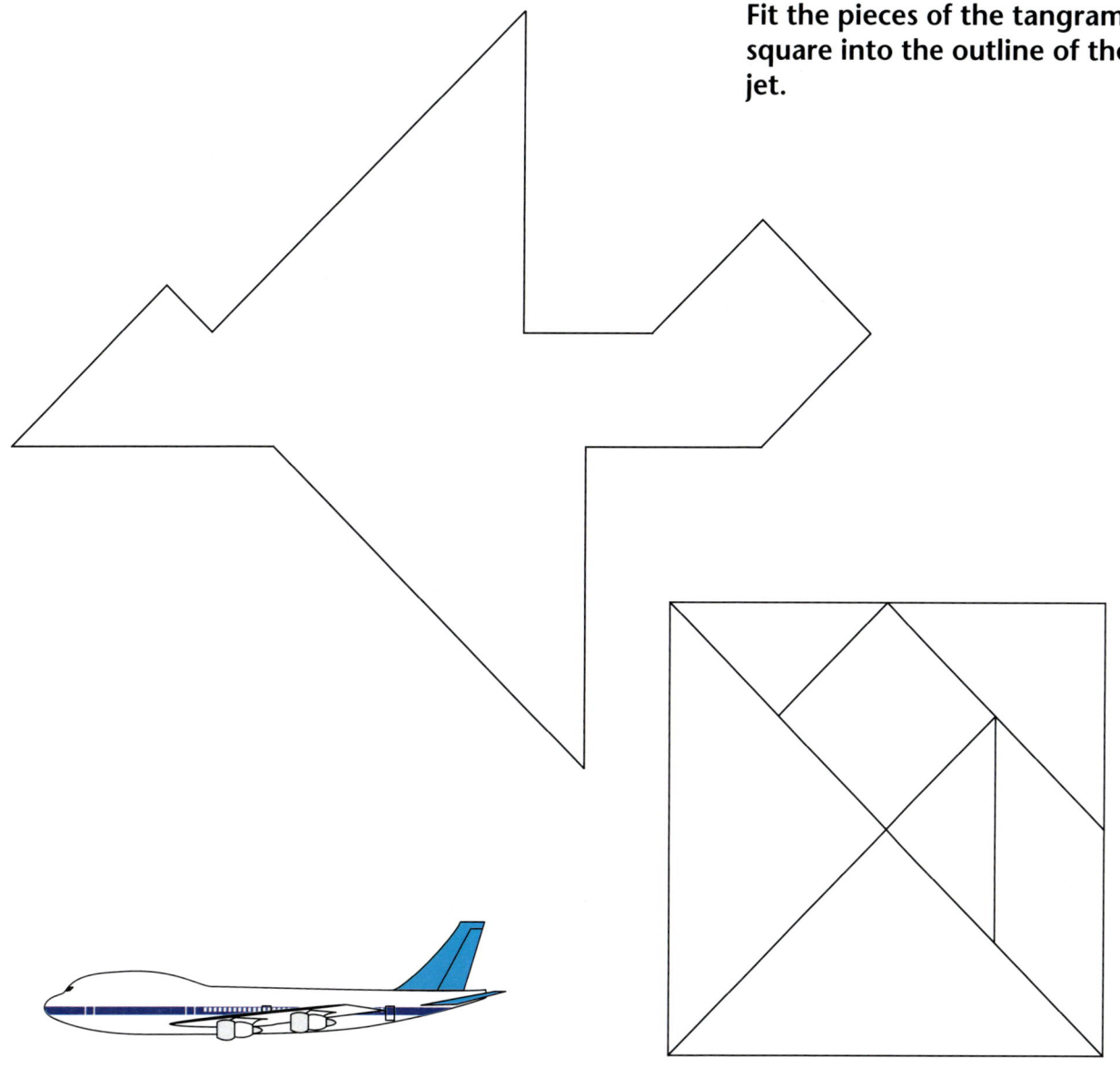

Fit the pieces of the tangram square into the outline of the jet.

Activity: To make a Mobius Strip

Highways

A strip that has only one side—like a highway— is a MOBIUS STRIP, named after August Ferdinand Mobius, a mathematician and astronomer who discovered it in the nineteenth century. You can make one following these directions.

Materials:
strip of paper 1 to 1 1/2 inches wide and about 11 to 12 inches long
tape
pencil
scissors

Process:
1. Hold one end of the paper strip flat and give the other end a half twist.

2. Fasten the ends of the strip together with tape.

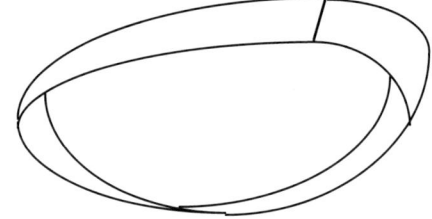

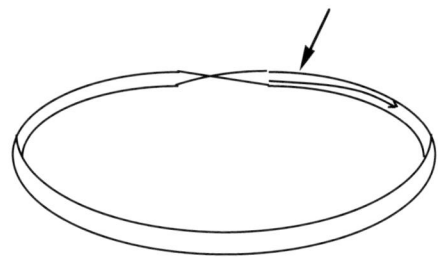

3. Take a pencil and start at some point about midway between the edges of the strip. Without lifting the pencil, trace a path around the strip.

4. Did you come back to your starting point without crossing an edge? Good for you! (This strip has just one side.)

5. Cut the strip along the path traced by the pencil. Do you have two separate strips? What has happened? Does it remind you of a highway? Repeat the process.

Activity: To use mathematics skills; to imagine the consequences of a decision

Traffic

"We wanted to learn about speed, traffic congestion, and pollution." (page 70)

In 1989 the world contained more than 555 million working motor vehicles, and around 28 million were being added to the total each year. Approximately how many working motor vehicles does the world currently contain? _____

Fill in the chart:

1989	*555 million*	1996	_____
1990	_____	1997	_____
1991	_____	1998	_____
1992	_____	1999	_____
1993	_____	2000	_____
1994	_____	2001	_____
1995	_____	2002	_____

This book has a copyright date of 1972. Do you think that the traffic problems in New York City have changed much in that time? How might they be different?

How would New York City be different today if Peter's suggestion of a citywide monorail system had been accepted and was up and running?

Activity: Vocabulary word recognition, grouping of letters into words and word usage

Vocabulary Word Search Puzzle

Circle the words in the word search puzzle. Write down the letters that have not been used, starting at the top and working left to right in each row. Group the letters into words to find out what decision it is that Peter makes.

Peter decides that he _____.

```
C O M B I N A T I O N H
O L A S H T G A N P E M
N H I A D Y E N S O M I
S E E E N P N T T L E C
I H F L N E C R A L R R
D B O A I T Y U L U G O
E O A V N U S M L T E S
R U G S E G M H O I N C
E F F U H D D G E O C O
D I S G U S T E D N Y P
I N G R E D I E N T S E
```

Words to Find

COMBINATION	EMERGENCY
AGENCY	MICROSCOPE
INSTALL	CONSIDERED
DISGUSTED	POLLUTION
TANTRUM	INGREDIENTS
CLIENTS	HELIUM
SHOVED	BASH
TYPE	FANG

Some other things to do with the words:

1. Put the words in alphabetical order.
2. Define half of the words.
3. Use half of the remaining words in sentences.

Activity: To make choices based on need and letter of the alphabet

Pack a Suitcase

"I was sitting on the bed watching my mother pack her suitcase." (page 82)

Do you remember playing "I'm Going to Pack My Trunk" when you were younger? THIS time you are going to pack a suitcase with items that you really could use, and that would really fit into a suitcase. Try to think of something for each letter of the alphabet. You may mention brand names to help match letters and items.

A _____   N _____

B _____   O _____

C _____   P _____

D _____   Q _____

E _____   R _____

F _____   S _____

G _____   T _____

H _____   U _____

I _____   V _____

J _____   W _____

K _____   X _____

L _____   Y _____

M _____   Z _____

Activity: To state and justify an opinion

Advertising

Mr. Hatcher takes the boys to the advertising agency. A television commercial will be made for the Toddle-Bike Company that afternoon. The following quotations have been made about advertising. Read them carefully. Choose one quotation and explain in your own words what it means.

1. "Advertising is what you do when you can't go see somebody."—**F. Cone**
2. "Few people at the beginning of the nineteenth century needed an adman to tell them what they wanted."—**J. K. Galbraith**
3. "I do not read advertisements—I would spend all my time wanting things." —**Archbishop of Canterbury**
4. "It used to be that people needed products to survive. Now products need people to survive."—**N. Johnson**
5. "Advertising has done more to cause the social unrest of the twentieth century than any other single factor."—**C. Barnes, Jr.**
6. "You can tell the ideals of a nation by its advertisements."—**N. Douglas**

I choose Quote # _____. I think it means _____

_____

_____

_____

_____

_____

_____

_____

_____

Name_____

Activity: To choose a favorite commercial and analyze its attributes

What Makes It Good?

Think about your favorite commercial. What is it that makes this commercial better than the rest? Is it one or more of the following—or something else? Circle the attributes that apply. Add any that don't appear.

music	characters in commercial	honesty/truthfulness
slogan	visual effects	simplicity
jingle	sound effects	humor

other_____   other_____

other_____   other_____

My favorite commercial is on: television____ radio____

The product it advertises is: _____

Use descriptive language to paint a word picture of your favorite commercial:

_____

_____

_____

_____

_____

_____

_____

_____

_____

Name_____

Activity: To define vocabulary words

Vocabulary Crossword Puzzle

On the list of **Words Used**, find a vocabulary word to match each of the **Across** and **Down** clues. Fit the words into the puzzle.

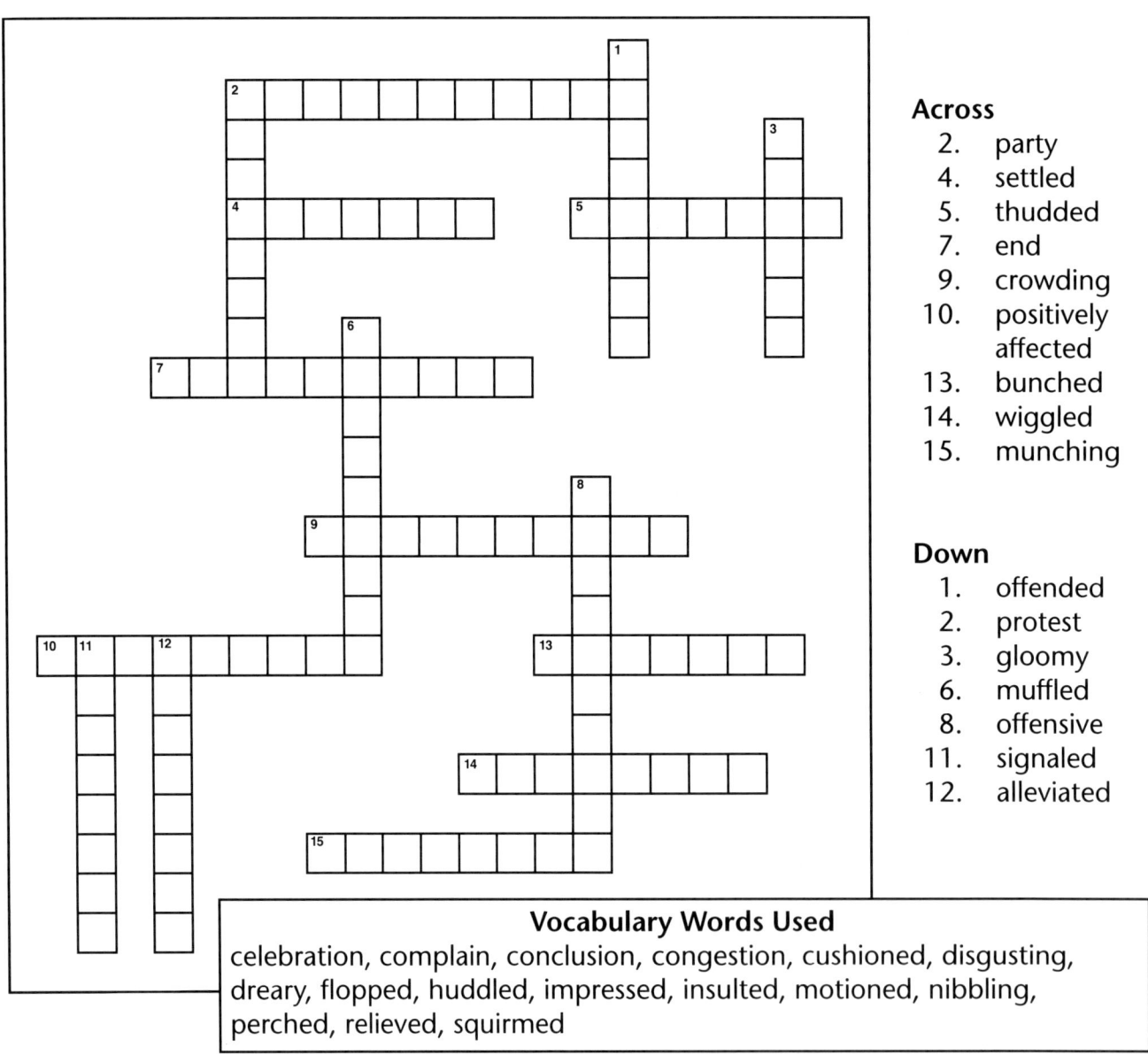

Across
2. party
4. settled
5. thudded
7. end
9. crowding
10. positively affected
13. bunched
14. wiggled
15. munching

Down
1. offended
2. protest
3. gloomy
6. muffled
8. offensive
11. signaled
12. alleviated

Vocabulary Words Used
celebration, complain, conclusion, congestion, cushioned, disgusting, dreary, flopped, huddled, impressed, insulted, motioned, nibbling, perched, relieved, squirmed

34

Activity: To make plans for a day

A Rainy Saturday

"The next day it rained. My father asked me how I'd like to go to the movies." (page 97)

Imagine that it is a rainy Saturday, and that you may choose what
you will do and what you will eat on that day, within the guidelines that follow:

1. The food you consume must be nutritious and varied. (You can't eat hamburgers and fries for breakfast, lunch, and dinner—but once is OK.)
2. Time spent on computer games, video arcade, etc. is limited to two hours total.
3. Television viewing time is limited to two hours total.
4. Paid-for outside entertainment, like a movie, is limited to one, the total cost not to exceed $10.00.

Things I'll Do…

What I'll Eat…

Activity: To make a comparison using a synonym or an antonym

Vocabulary Review

vanish	conclusion	miserable
insulted	dreary	disgusting

Complete each of the following comparisons using one of the vocabulary words from the list above.

Sample: GOOD is to BAD as HOT is to COLD.

1. STAY is to REMAIN as _____is to DISAPPEAR.

2. GLAD is to HAPPY as _____ is to OFFENDED.

3. BETTER is to WORSE as _____ is to BEGINNING.

4. HERE is to THERE as _____ is to CHEERFUL.

5. LOSE is to FIND as _____ is to ATTRACTIVE.

6. SCARED is to FRIGHTENED as _____ is to WRETCHED.

Make up three comparisons of your own. You do not have to use vocabulary words.

7. _____ is to _____ as _____ is to _____.

8. _____ is to _____ as _____ is to _____.

9. _____ is to _____ as _____ is to _____.

Activity: To design a home for Dribble that would be Fudge-proof

A New Home

"I ran to the dresser to check on Dribble. He wasn't there!" (page 109)

Perhaps a newly designed home could have prevented the demise of Dribble. Can you design one that would be Fudge-proof? Make an illustration of your design, and explain how it would keep Fudge out and Dribble in.

Fudge-proof Turtle Home Design by_____

How it works: _____

_____

_____

_____

_____

_____

_____

Directions: Write a brief summary of the story. Give your opinion of the story. What do you like and dislike about it? Why? What has reading the story given you? Would you recommend it to others? Why or why not?

_____

_____

_____

_____

_____

_____

_____

_____

_____

_____

_____

_____

_____

_____

_____

_____

_____

_____

_____

_____

_____

_____

To The Teacher

The concluding activity may be used as the final test for the novel unit. The student is asked to write a brief summary of the story, and to express an opinion about it. The student is also asked to describe what the story has given to him/her.

The following pages may be used as quiz pages if the teacher so desires:

a) Chapter 1, Worksheet #3, Turtles. To read for information.

b) Chapter 2, Worksheet #6, Pots and Pans. To use reasoning skills.

c) Chapter 4, Worksheet #16, Your Environment. To use mathematics skills.

d) Chapter 4, Worksheet #17, Pollution Crossword Puzzle. To match words with definitions; to learn more about pollution.

e) Chapter 4, Worksheet #18, Playground. To use the letters of one word to form others; spelling practice.

f) Chapter 8, Worksheet #28, Vocabulary Word Search Puzzle. Vocabulary word recognition.

g) Chapter 9, Worksheet #32, Vocabulary Crossword Puzzle. To define vocabulary words.

h) Chapter 10, Worksheet #34, Vocabulary Review. To make a comparison using a synonym or an antonym of a vocabulary word.

Comprehension quizzes follow.

Name_____

Directions: Read the information and fill in the blank space with a word, words or phrase that will make the information given complete and true to the story.

Sample: The name of this novel is _Tales of a Fourth Grade Nothing_ .

1. Peter Hatcher wins a _____ at a birthday party.

2. Peter names the turtle _____.

3. Peter's father is in the _____ business. The family lives in an apartment in _____ City.

4. Peter's biggest problem is his little _____, whose nickname is_____.

5. Fudge decides to start eating again because his father tells him to eat or to _____ his cereal!

6. Peter and Jimmy like to play in _____ after school. They have some favorite _____ there.

7. Fudge decides that he is a bird. He jumps off of the _____at the park. His two _____ are knocked out.

8. Fudge has a _____ party. Peter learns that young children like to jump off of the _____.

9. Peter has to pretend to like _____ shoes, so that Fudge will get some.

10. After a day with Fudge, Peter decides that he will _____ do it again!

Directions: Read the information and fill in the blank space with a word, words or phrase that will make the information given complete and true to the story.

Sample: The name of this novel is _Tales of a Fourth Grade Nothing_ .

1. The topic of the report to be done by Peter, Jimmy and Sheila is _____.

2. Fudge ruins the _____ done by Peter and Jimmy.

3. After Fudge cuts his _____ with the scissors in Peter's room, Mr.

   Hatcher brings home a _____ for Peter's door.

4. Fudge gets to make a _____ while the boys are with their father at

   work. Fudge misbehaves, and _____ saves the day!

5. Mr. Hatcher takes Peter and Fudge to see a movie about _____. Fudge

   moves up to the front of the theater because he wants to _____them.

6. Mr. Hatcher cooks an _____ for dinner. It tastes _____! They

   have _____ sandwiches instead.

7. Dribble is missing. Fudge has _____ the turtle.

8. Peter's parents buy him a new pet. It is a _____. Peter names it

   _____.

Answer Key

Worksheet #1: 16 triangles

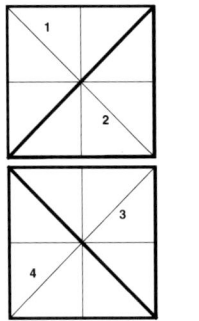 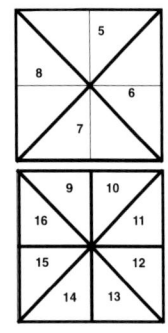 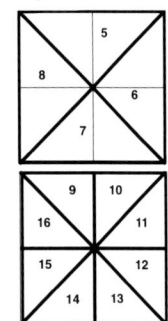

Worksheet #2: Tangram Turtle

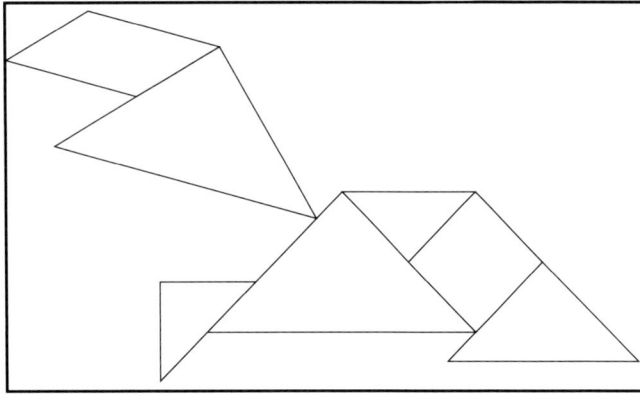

Worksheet #17: Pollution Crossword

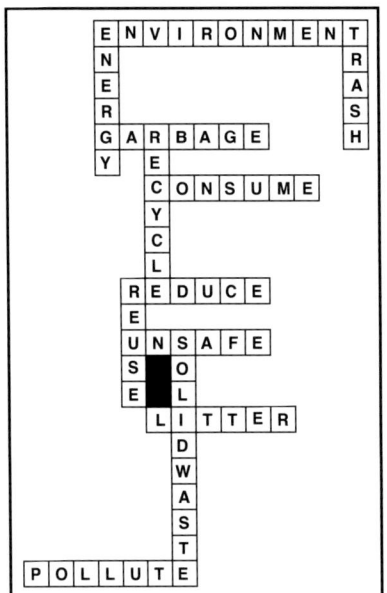

Worksheet #3:
1. T
2. F
3. T
4. T
5. T
6. F
7. T
8. T

Worksheet #16:
waste—week: 24.5 pounds
31 days: 108.5 pounds
365 days: 1,277.50 pounds

paper—week: 12.25 pounds
31 days: 54.25 pounds
365 days: 638.75 pounds

Worksheet #18: (samples)
PLAYGROUND

PLAY	POUND	DROP	PAN
YARN	GROUND	ROUND	LOP
AN	DARN	DAY	LAP
NAG	PLAN	GRAY	GAP
DRAG	GRAND	LAY	RAP
RAG	AND	RAY	NAP
RAN	LAND		

CENTRAL PARK

LARK	RACK	RAN	RACE
NECK	RAP	TRACK	CENT
TAN	ACE	PECK	TRAP
LACK	RENT	PAN	PACE
LAP	PEN	PACK	LENT
CAN	TRACE	NAP	TEN

Worksheet #24: Tangram Sailboat

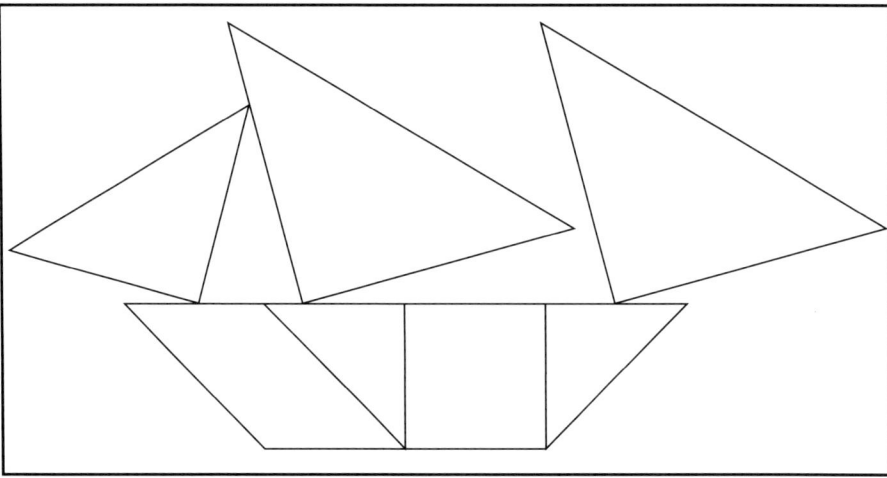

Worksheet #25: Tangram Jet

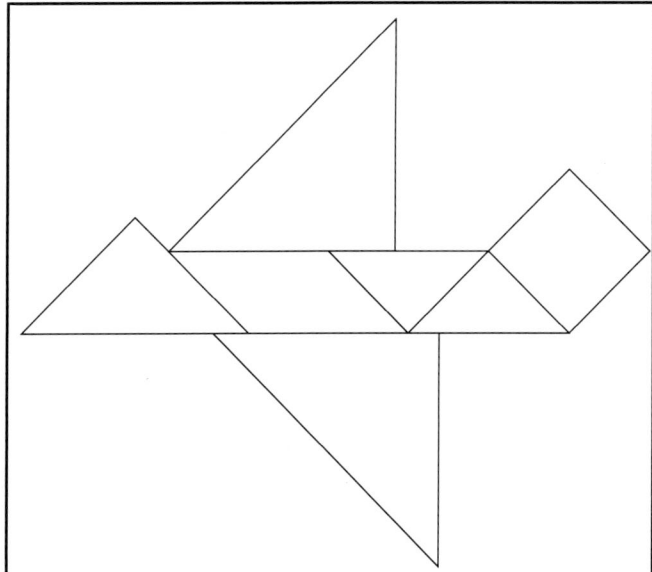

Worksheet #27

1989	555 million	1996	751 million
1990	583 million	1997	779 million
1991	611 million	1998	807 million
1992	639 million	1999	835 million
1993	667 million	2000	863 million
1994	695 million	2001	891 million
1995	723 million	2002	919 million

Worksheet #28: Vocabulary Word Search

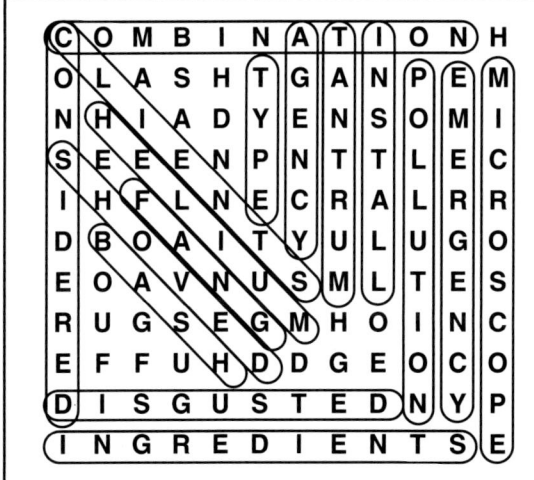

Peter decides that he **HAS HAD ENOUGH OF FUDGE.**

Worksheet #32: Vocabulary Crossword

Worksheet #34:

1 VANISH
2 INSULTED
3 CONCLUSION
4 DREARY
5 DISGUSTING
6 MISERABLE

Note: Students' answers to some quiz questions may vary from those listed below but still be correct.

Quiz #1
1. turtle
2. Dribble
3. advertising/New York
4. brother/Fudge
5. wear
6. Central Park/rocks
7. jungle gym/teeth
8. birthday/furniture
9. saddle
10. never

Quiz #2
1. transportation
2. poster
3. hair/lock
4. commercial/Peter
5. bears/touch
6. omelette/awful/ peanut butter
7. swallowed
8. dog/Turtle

Notes